WORDS
TO SAY
I LOVE YOU

WORDS
TO SAY
I LOVE YOU

COMPILED BY SARAH HOGGETT
DESIGNED BY DAVID FORDHAM

CICO BOOKS
LONDON NEW YORK

Published by CICO Books
An imprint of Ryland Peters and Small Ltd

20–21 Jockey's Fields
London WC1R 4BW

519 Broadway, 5th Floor
New York, NY 10012

10 9 8 7 6 5 4 3 2 1

This edition © CICO Books 2008

A CIP catalog record for this book is available from the Library of Congress
and the British Library.

US ISBN-13: 978 1 906094 23 2
US ISBN-10: 1 906094 23 3

UK ISBN-13: 978 1 906094 22 5
UK ISBN-10: 1 906094 22 5

Printed in China

Compiled by Sarah Hoggett
Designed by David Fordham

CONTENTS

LOVE
&
ROMANCE

INTRODUCTION

Being in love is a magical feeling: Your heart misses a beat when that certain someone walks into the room, you catch sight of yourself in a mirror and realize there's a big, soppy grin on your face for no apparent reason, and even on the dullest of days you feel as if the sun is shining on everything you do!

It's a fair bet that, over the course of human history, more ink has been expended on writing words of love than on any other subject. Telling the object of your affections how you feel, however, is not always easy. So if you're racking your brains for a suitable verse for a Valentine's Day card or an amorous sentiment for a *billet-doux*, then look no further!

WORDS TO SAY I LOVE YOU

contains over 70 memorable and heart-felt quotations, spanning a period of more than 4,000 years from ancient Sumeria right up to the present day.

Philosophers and poets from the ancient world take their place alongside the 14th-century Hafiz of Persia and such all-time greats as Shakespeare and John Donne. You will find the military genius Napoleon Bonaparte in romantic mode as he writes to his lover, Joséphine. And more contemporary musings can be found in the words of American humorist and poet Don Marquis and Liverpudlian legend John Lennon.

Whether you're suffering the bitter-sweet pangs of your first romance or declaring your devotion to a life-long partner, *Words to Say I Love You* contains something to suit all moods and mindsets, from the love-lorn and lonely to the lusciously lustful.

> **" Since *love* grows within you, so beauty grows. For *love* is the beauty of the soul. "**
>
> St Augustine (354–430)

"TRUE *love* COMES QUIETLY, WITHOUT BANNERS OR FLASHING LIGHTS. IF YOU HEAR **BELLS**, GET YOUR EARS CHECKED."

Erich Segal (1937–)

8

WHAT IS LOVE?

"LOVE
IS LIKE THE
MEASLES;
WE ALL HAVE TO
GO THROUGH IT."

Jerome K. Jerome (1859–1927)

10

66 *'Tis very much like*
LIGHT,
a thing that everybody knows, and yet none can tell what
to make of it:
'Tis not

MONEY, FORTUNE, JOYNTURE, RAVING, STABBING, HANGING, ROMANCING, FLOUNCING, SWEARING, RAMPING, DESIRING, FIGHTING, DYING,

though all those
HAVE BEEN, ARE, & STILL WILL BE
mistaken and miscalled for it. 99

Definition of love, from *The Ladies' Dictionary* (1694)

"LOVE
is the wine
OF EXISTENCE."

Henry Ward Beecher (1813–1887)

*"That Love is **all** there is,*
*Is **all** we know of Love."*

Emily Dickinson (1830–1886)

"

WHAT LOVE IS, IF THOU WOULDST BE TAUGHT,

THE HEART MUST TEACH   ALONE —

TWO SOULS WITH BUT A SINGLE THOUGHT,

TWO HEARTS THAT BEAT AS ONE. "

SOULS

HEARTS

Friedrich Halm (1806–1871)

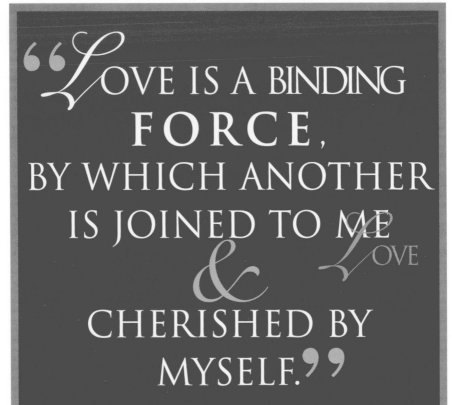

"LOVE IS A BINDING **FORCE**, BY WHICH ANOTHER IS JOINED TO ME & *LOVE* CHERISHED BY MYSELF."

Thomas Aquinas (c. 1225–1274)

" O, love, love, love!
Love is like a dizziness;
It winna [will not] let a poor body
Gang [go] about his biziness! "

James Hogg (1770–1835), 'Love is like a dizziness'

" LOVE IS A FANCLUB
WITH ONLY TWO FANS. "

Adrian Henri (1932–2000)

"LOVE LOOKS NOT WITH THE EYES, BUT WITH THE MIND; AND THEREFORE IS WING'D CUPID PAINTED BLIND."

William Shakespeare (1564–1616)

"LIKE I'VE ALWAYS SAID, LOVE WOULDN'T BE BLIND IF THE BRAILLE WEREN'T SO DAMNED MUCH FUN."

Armistead Maupin (1944–)

"We've got this gift of LOVE,
but LOVE is like a precious plant.

You can't just accept it and leave it in
the cupboard or just think it's going to get
on by itself. You've got to keep watering it.
You've got to really look after it
and nurture it."

John Lennon (1940–1980)

LOVE
is a temporary madness.

It erupts like an earthquake and then
subsides. And when it subsides…
you have to work out whether your
roots have become so *entwined together*
that it is inconceivable that you should
ever P A R T. … We had roots that
grew towards each other
underground, and when all the pretty
blossom had fallen from our branches
we found that we were
ONE tree and not **TWO**.

Louis de Bernières (1954–)

THE POWER OF LOVE

"LOVE

CONQUERS ALL THINGS: LET US, TOO, GIVE IN TO

LOVE"

Virgil (70–19 BCE)

"Love wing'd my Hopes and taught me how to fly.

Anonymous

NOTHING TAKES THE TASTE OUT OF PEANUT BUTTER QUITE LIKE UNREQUITED LOVE.

Charlie Brown in "Peanuts" comic strip, created by Charles M. Schultz

IF GRASS CAN GROW THROUGH CEMENT, LOVE CAN FIND YOU AT EVERY TIME IN YOUR LIFE.

Cher (1946–)

"PEOPLE WHO ARE **NOT** IN LOVE **FAIL** TO UNDERSTAND HOW AN INTELLIGENT MAN CAN **SUFFER** BECAUSE OF A VERY **ORDINARY** WOMAN. THIS IS LIKE BEING SURPRISED THAT ANYONE SHOULD BE **STRICKEN** WITH CHOLERA BECAUSE OF A CREATURE SO **INSIGNIFICANT** AS THE COMMON BACILLUS.**"**

Marcel Proust (1871–1922)

" LOVE WILL DRAW AN **ELEPHANT** THROUGH A KEY-HOLE. **"**

Samuel Richardson (1689–1761)

" As soon go kindle FIRE *with* SNOW, *as seek to quench the* FIRE *of* LOVE *with words.* **"**

William Shakespeare (1564–1616)

"LIFE *without* LOVE

IS LIKE A TREE *without* BLOSSOMS OR FRUIT."

Kahlil Gibran (1883–1931)

" At the touch of
LOVE,
everyone becomes a *poet*."

Plato (?427–347 BCE)

" *If I meet*
you suddenly, I can't
speak — my tongue is B RO K EN;
a thin flame runs under
my skin; seeing nothing,
thin flame
hearing only my own ears
drumming, I drip with sweat;
drip
trembling shakes my body
drip
and I turn paler *than*
drip
dry grass. At such times
drip
death isn't far from me. "

Sappho
(6th century BCE)

25

"TO LOVE SOMEONE ♥ DEEPLY GIVES YOU STRENGTH.

♥ BEING LOVED BY SOMEONE DEEPLY GIVES YOU COURAGE."

Lao Tzu (?604–531 BCE)

26

HOW DO
I LOVE THEE?

"Thou art my **LIFE**, my **LOVE**, my **HEART**,
The very eyes of me:
And hast command of every part
To **LIVE** and **DIE** for thee."

Robert Herrick (1591–1674)

"My bounty is as boundless as the sea,
My love as **DEEP**. The **more** I give to thee
The **more** I have, for both are infinite."

William Shakespeare (1564–1616)

I WILL COVER *you* WITH LOVE WHEN NEXT I SEE *you*, WITH CARESSES, WITH ECSTASY. I WANT TO GORGE *you* WITH ALL THE JOYS OF THE FLESH, SO THAT *you* FAINT AND DIE. I WANT *you* TO BE AMAZED BY ME, AND TO CONFESS TO YOURSELF THAT *you* HAD NEVER EVEN DREAMED OF SUCH TRANSPORTS.... WHEN *you* ARE OLD, I WANT *you* TO RECALL THOSE FEW HOURS, I WANT YOUR DRY BONES TO QUIVER WITH JOY WHEN *you* THINK OF THEM. Gustave Flaubert (1821–1880)

"I AM YOUR CLAY.
YOU ARE MY CLAY.
IN LIFE WE SHARE A SINGLE QUILT.
IN DEATH WE WILL SHARE ONE COFFIN."

Kuan Tao-sheng (1262–1319)

"DO NOT SMILE TO YOURSELF
LIKE A GREEN MOUNTAIN
WITH A CLOUD DRIFTING ACROSS IT.
PEOPLE WILL KNOW WE ARE IN LOVE."

Ōtomo no Sakano-e no Iratsume (c. 700–750)

"HOW DO I LOVE THEE?
LET ME COUNT THE WAYS.
I LOVE THEE TO THE
DEPTH and BREADTH and
H E I G H T
MY SOUL
CAN REACH."

Elizabeth Barrett Browning (1806–1861)

Here are fruits, flowers, leaves, and branches, And here is my heart which beats ONLY *for you.* ♥

Paul Verlaine (1844–1896)

You are MY HEART, ♥
MY LIFE, ♥
MY ONE AND ONLY ♥
THOUGHT. ♥

Sir Arthur Conan Doyle (1859–1930)

32

"WHATEVER OUR SOULS ARE MADE OF, *his & mine* ARE THE *same.*"

Emily Brontë (1818–1848)

"I LOVE YOU ♥ AS ♥ NEW ENGLANDERS LOVE PIE."

Don Marquis (1878–1937)

"I love thee – I love thee,
'Tis all that I can say
It is my vision in the night,
My dreaming in the day."

Thomas Hood (1799–1845)

" I CAN NO LONGER THINK OF ANYTHING BUT **YOU**. IN SPITE OF MYSELF, **MY** IMAGINATION CARRIES **ME** TO **YOU**.

I *Grasp* YOU,

I *Kiss* YOU,

I *Caress* YOU,

A THOUSAND OF THE MOST AMOROUS CARESSES TAKE POSSESSION OF **ME**. **"**

Honoré de Balzac (1799–1850)

"*I*, MY SWEET & DARLING ONE,
WITH WHOM *I* WOULD SPEAK HONEY —
YOUTH, *I* AM IN LOVE WITH YOU!"

Kubatum (Sumerian priestess, c. 2032 BCE)

"*Eros has shaken my thoughts, like a wind among highland oaks.*"

Sappho (6th century BCE)

"KNOW, *my love,* THAT I SHOULD LIKE TO CALL YOU A THIEF, BECAUSE YOU HAVE STOLEN MY HEART..."

" When my self is not with you, it is nowhere."

WITHOUT YOU, EVERY MORNING WOULD FEEL LIKE BACK GOING TO WORK AFTER A HOLIDAY.

Adrian Henri (1932–2000)

"I'll love you dear, I'll love you

Till China&Africa meet,

And the river jumps over the mountain

And the salmon sing in the street."

W.H. Auden (1907–1973)

" "
Doubt that the stars are FIRE,
Doubt that the SUN doth move,
Doubt truth to be a liar,
But never *doubt* I LOVE. " "

William Shakespeare (1564–1616)

LOVE'S ENCHANTMENT

IS IT POSSIBLE THAT *Love* SHOULD OF A SUDDEN TAKE SUCH HOLD?

William Shakespeare (1564–1616)

" *There is a Lady sweet and kind,*
Was never face so pleased my mind;
I did but see her passing by,
And yet I love her till I die. "

Anonymous

"WHERE BOTH DELIBERATE,
THE LOVE IS SLIGHT,
WHO EVER LOVED,
THAT LOVED NOT
AT FIRST SIGHT?"

Christopher Marlowe (1564–1593)

43

"BUT TO SEE HER, WAS TO LOVE HER;
LOVE BUT HER, AND LOVE FOR EVER."

Robert Burns (1759–1796)

"NO,
there's nothing
HALF SO SWEET
in life as love's young dream. "

Thomas Moore (1779–1852)

"AH, HOW *sweet* IT IS TO L♥VE!
AH, HOW *gay* IS YOUNG *Desire*!
AND WHAT *pleasing* PAINS WE PROVE
WHEN WE FIRST APPROACH *Love's fire*!
PAINS OF L♥VE BE *sweeter* FAR
THAN ALL OTHER *pleasures* ARE."

John Dryden (1631–1700)

" *I* WISH *I* HAD THE GIFT
OF MAKING RHYMES, FOR
METHINKS THERE IS POETRY
IN MY HEAD AND ♥HEART
SINCE *I* HAVE BEEN
in Love WITH YOU. **"**

Nathaniel Hawthorne (1804–1864)

"At one glance
I love you
With a thousand hearts"

Mihri Hatun (?–1506)

"THE MAGIC OF FIRST ♥ LOVE IS OUR IGNORANCE THAT IT CAN EVER END."

END
END
END
END

Benjamin Disraeli
(1804–1881)

"HOW ON EARTH ARE YOU EVER GOING TO EXPLAIN IN TERMS OF CHEMISTRY & PHYSICS SO **IMPORTANT** A BIOLOGICAL PHENOMENON AS FIRST LOVE?**"**

Albert Einstein (1879–1955)

KISSES....
AND MORE

"*Kissing* is like drinking salted water. You drink, and your thirst *increases*."

Chinese proverb

" GIVE ME A *kiss*, AND TO
THAT *kiss* A SCORE;
THEN TO THAT TWENTY,
ADD A HUNDRED MORE;
A THOUSAND TO THAT
HUNDRED; SO *kiss* ON,
TO MAKE THAT THOUSAND
UP A MILLION;
TREBLE THAT MILLION, AND
WHEN THAT IS DONE,
LET'S *kiss* AFRESH, AS WHEN
WE FIRST BEGUN. "

Robert Herrick (1592–1674)

"i like my body when it is with your body. It is so quite a new thing. Muscles better and nerves more.

"LICENCE MY ROVING HANDS,
AND LET THEM GO,
BEFORE, BEHIND, BETWEEN,
ABOVE, BELOW."

John Donne (1573–1631)

"A *kiss* IS A LOVELY TRICK DESIGNED BY NATURE TO **STOP** SPEECH WHEN WORDS BECOME SUPERFLUOUS."

Ingrid Bergman (1915–1982)

"LET HIM *kiss* ME WITH THE *kisses* OF HIS MOUTH! FOR YOUR LOVE IS **BETTER** THAN WINE."

Bible: *Song of Solomon* 1:2.

" UNTIL THEN, *mio dolce amor,* A THOUSAND KISSES; BUT GIVE ME NONE IN RETURN, FOR THEY SET MY BLOOD ON FIRE. FIRE. FIRE. "

Napoleon Bonaparte (1769–1821)

"*Soul meets soul on lovers' lips.*"

Percy Bysshe Shelley (1792–1822)

ONCE HE DREW WITH ONE LONG *kiss* MY WHOLE SOUL THROUGH MY *lips,* AS SUNLIGHT DRINKETH DEW.

Alfred Lord Tennyson (1809–1892)

"I LOVE YOUR *lips*
WHEN THEY'RE
wet with wine

AND *red* WITH
A *wicked desire*."

Ella Wheeler Wilcox (1855–1919)

"One regret, dear world, that I am determined not to have when I lie on my deathbed is that I did not kiss you enough."

Hafiz of Persia (1321–1389)

" FRIENDS,
YOU ARE LUCKY YOU CAN TALK
ABOUT WHAT YOU DID AS
♥ LOVERS:
THE TRICKS, LAUGHTER, THE
♥ WORDS,
THE ECSTASY.
AFTER MY DARLING PUT HIS
♥ HAND ON THE KNOT
OF MY DRESS,
I SWEAR I REMEMBER
♥ NOTHING. "
    NOTHING
        NOTHING

Vidya (fl. c. 700–1050)

59

"WHATEVER PATCH OF LIMB
HE GAZES ON
WITH UNBLINKING EYES,
I COVER UP
BUT I WANT HIM TO SEE IT
ALL ANYWAY."

Hla Stavhana (South Indian king, c. 50 CE)

60

"*My sweet one, wash me with honey —*

In the bed that is filled with honey,
Let us enjoy our love.
Lion, let me give you my caresses,

My sweet one, wash me with honey."

Kubatum (Sumerian priestess, c. 2032 BCE)

"Stay, O sweet and **DO NOT** RISE!
The light that shines comes from thine eyes;
The day breaks **NOT**: it is my heart,
Because that **YOU** & I must part.
Stay! or else my joys will **DIE**
AND PERISH in their infancy."

John Donne (1573–1631)

"Coming to *kiss* her lips, *(such grace I found)*,
Meseem'd, I *smelt* a garden of sweet flowers..."

Edmund Spenser (1552?–1599)

ACKNOWLEDGMENTS

The publishers are grateful to the following for permission to reproduce extracts from works in copyright.

p. 15 Adrian Henri: From 'Love is...', copyright © 1967 Adrian Henri. Reproduced by permission of the estate of Adrian Henri, c/o Rogers, Coleridge & White Ltd., 20 Powis Mews, London W11 1JN.

p. 16 Armistead Maupin: From *Maybe the Moon*, reproduced by permission of HarperCollins Publishers Ltd.

p. 18 Louis de Bernieres: From *Captain Corelli's Mandolin*, published by Vintage (May 1995). Reprinted by permission of The Random House Group Ltd and Random House Inc.

p. 38 Adrian Henri: From 'Without you', copyright © 1967 Adrian Henri. Reproduced by permission of the estate of Adrian Henri, c/o Rogers, Coleridge & White Ltd., 20 Powis Mews, London W11 1JN.

p. 39 W.H. Auden: From 'As I Walked Out One Evening', reproduced by permission of Faber & Faber and Random House Inc.

p. 52, E.E. Cummings: From "i like my body when it is with your" reprinted from COMPLETE POEMS 1904–1962, by E.E. Cummings, edited by George J. Firmage, by permission of W.W. Norton & Company. Copyright © 1991 by the Trustees for the E.E. Cummings Trust and George James Firmage.

Every effort has been made to contact copyright holders and to acknowledge sources, but the publishers would be glad to hear of any omissions.

INDEX OF AUTHORS